Ancestral Healing

Gateway to Synchronicity

by Joseph Knapp

Blue Lotus Press

Dripping Springs, Texas

Copyright © 2009 by Joseph Knapp

All rights reserved.

No part of this publication may be reproduced or transmitted in any form, by any means, electronic or mechanical, including photocopy, recording, or media information storage or retrieval systems now known, or to be invented, without written permission from the writer and publisher, except by a reviewer who wishes to quote brief passages in connection with a review written for inclusion in an educational publication or radio or TV broadcast.

ISBN 978-1-936135-51-6   (ISBN10 1-936135-51-5)

Published by Blue Lotus Press
A division of Sacred Ecology 33
118 Overlook Cove,
Dripping Springs, TX. 78620
http://www.sacredecology33.org

The information in this book is for educational purposes only and makes no claim that its content or products are meant to treat, diagnose, cure or prevent disease. Nor should the information replace the advice of your doctor or health care practitioner. No information obtained here should be relied on as the basis for treating or diagnosing conditions, symptoms, or illness and all queries should be directed to your health professional. If you have a medical condition, we recommend that you consult a health-care professional.

CONTENTS
PUBLISHER'S NOTE I
FOREWORD III
INTRODUCTION VII
   Why is it Necessary to Work With Our Ancestors? x
   Ancestral Healing Ceremonies and Rituals xiii
CHAPTER ONE: 1
AFRICAN ANCESTRAL TRADITIONS 1
CHAPTER TWO: 5
NATIVE/INDIGENOUS ANCESTRAL TRADITIONS ... 5
   Ancestor Beliefs in 9
   Hawaiian Religious Traditions 9
CHAPTER THREE: 13
FAR EAST ANCESTRAL TRADITIONS 13
   Ancestor Beliefs in Japanese Religious Traditions 16
   Ancestor Beliefs in Chinese Religious Traditions 22
CHAPTER FOUR: 25
WESTERN ANCESTRAL TRADITIONS 25
   Ancestor Beliefs in Jewish Religious Traditions 25
   Ancestor Beliefs in Christian Religious Traditions 27
   Ancestor Beliefs in Islamic Religious Traditions 29
CHAPTER FIVE: 31
NEW AGE ANCESTRAL COMMUNICATION 31
CHAPTER SIX: 35
STORIES OF ANCESTRAL HEALING 35
CHAPTER SEVEN: 41

ANCESTRAL CEREMONIES AND RITUALS 41
    Creating Ancestral Connections 42
    Ceremonies 43
    Prayers 44
    Offerings 45
    Incense 46
    Candles 46
    Altars 47
    Facilitating Ancestral Connections on Your Own 48
    Conclusion 49
APPENDIX 1 53
SACRED ECOLOGY 33 53
APPENDIX 2 57
WHO IS JOSEPH? 57
APPENDIX 3 61
PATH OF THE SACRED HEALER 61
APPENDIX 4 67
SELECTED MIRACLES OF SPIRITUAL INTERVENTION
... 67
CONTACT INFORMATION FOR JOSEPH KNAPP 72
BIBLIOGRAPHY 73

Publisher's Note

We are happy to release this small book on the rare art form of Ancestral Healing. Joseph Knapp not only has the ability to connect and communicate with those who have passed away into the realms beyond earthly life, but he also has the ability to perform direct healing on the souls of your loved ones. This is one of the best kept secrets, known only to a few who have heard about Joseph through word of mouth and been fortunate enough to experience this form of spiritual intervention work.

For the past 40 years Joseph has been quietly perfecting his craft and profession. With the release of *Ancestral Healing: Gateway to Synchronicity*—and more to come—Joseph's rare and powerful gifts to universally help people live clearer, happier self-empowered lives for themselves, their children, and other family members are now being brought to light.

Joseph Knapp and Blue Lotus Press want to thank the people who have helped with research, editing, creative input and encouragement such as Nestor Abanil, Alison Monfort, Lynn Shook, and Erika Celeste. We also extend our gratitude to the friends, clients, and students who kindly gave testimony to their own personal healing over the years in working with Joseph. Thanks to Michael Allen for his assistance in layout and formatting for his work and artistic contributions on the book cover.

Foreword

Before meeting Joseph, I had little interest in knowing about my heritage or the idea that my ancestors could have an impact on my life. I was more focused on the external world of career development, raising a family, and building the typical American dream. My life was not unique. It had its milestones and accomplishments, bumps, and disappointments along the way until a time came when there were more disappointments, unexplainable losses, and a deep sadness surrounding what others perceived to be a life of success and happiness.

I consulted my medical doctor regarding my depression and confusion and to my surprise he offered to take me to meet a man he called Joseph, a Spiritual Master and Healer who was visiting from California. He highly recommended Joseph, having experienced his work and thought he may be able to provide a different approach to viewing my situation. I must admit I reluctantly accepted, and attended only because of my doctor's recommendation.

Upon meeting Joseph, I saw a typical looking young man from Southern California. He appeared rather ordinary, and nothing like what I had envisioned as a Spiritual Master, until he introduced himself. His presence was that of a humble monk, but his eyes shown with a depth and wisdom beyond my immediate comprehension. A spiritual turning point took place that evening that opened my heart to an inner journey and world previously unknown to me. Since then Joseph's wisdom, his teachings in the Rasik (Yogic) tradition and Ancestral Healings have been a transforming experience for me. My husband and adult son saw a remarkable change in me, and they too started working with Joseph. My friends, colleagues, doctors, and healing practitioners began attending his group ancestral work or working with him privately.

I personally witnessed many remarkable healings through his group spiritual intervention work. Some had long-term, difficult associations with family members that were transformed into caring, loving relationships. My husband had a declining heart condition that was returned to normal function and verified by his medical doctors. This was a miracle beyond what I thought possible at the time. I have witnessed Joseph help change many situations for the better. The best way to describe this work is that psycho-spiritual events occur for each person allowing love and healing to be exchanged between the physical and spiritual realms.

I have learned over the years these transformative experiences are spiritual breakthroughs and gifts of grace that provide a sacred space in which to release, renew, and grow spiritually, physically, and emotionally. In simpler terms, it is like cleaning out one's closet of things that have been forgotten or emotionally held on to but no longer are useful. They often take up precious space and leave little or no room for anything new and more wonderful. This "stuff" we carry in the physical world and may continue to carry with us upon death into the spiritual realm are karmic impingements. As they are removed, so too is our psycho-physical burden, and we are renewed in body, mind, and soul.

Joseph's years of deep spiritual training with rare masters and his knowledge about other ancestral cultures open us to a new way of viewing our own lives' conditions and experiences. He offers a profound insight into our karmic link with our ancestors and provides a means for deep sacred healing.

The spiritual intervention work of Ancestral Healing is an extraordinary gift that has exponential possibilities and benefits. Joseph has written *Ancestral Healing: Gateway to Synchronicity* to open the way for us to gain greater spiritual understanding and healing.

Lynn Shook, *(executive consultant to global corporations and avid student of the mystic traditions and healing arts). June 2, 2009.*

Introduction

Have you ever driven by a house that is centuries old or perhaps touched an ancient work of art and felt energy still residing there? It's as if the walls have kept a silent record of passing generations, as if the artist's spirit were imprinted between brushstrokes or carved into ancient curves of marble. Similarly, we are canvases which bear the imprint of our ancestors' spirits. We are the marble through which their love, hate, desires, and unfulfilled dreams run like aged veins. Whatever their crimes, whatever their sadness, their emotional attachments, or pain they will continue to affect us, our children, and our children's children until the cycle is broken. A powerful methodology to cleanse the negative karma resulting from our bloodline is termed Ancestral Healing.

Ancestors play a part in our circumstances in life. They influence us in ways of which we may be unaware. This is called ancestor impingement. On the negative side they sometimes want to get satisfaction through us, continue gripes in the family, revenge, influence us with their personal opinions in regards to what work we should do, whom we choose as romantic partners, and/or how we go about living our lives. In some instances they fight amongst themselves and affect our ability to experience moment-to-moment peace.

Right now, we have a special opportunity to create a beneficial mutual relationship for healing and evolution. Our ancestors have a tendency to want to live through us, just like our parents want the best for us, yet have a limited view and sometimes try to superimpose their ideas of what is good for us. Therefore, this pressure from our ancestors can be a great hindrance to our own fulfillment.

Ancestral healing is a process by which Joseph makes contact with a client's ancestors and heals them of the different misunderstandings and discordant, negative attitudes, traumas, and unfulfilled desires. The word 'ancestors' includes each of us. We are the future ancestors for our progeny. In the traditional sense it also includes our parents, their brothers and sisters, our parents' parents, their brothers and sisters, our parents' parents' parents and their brothers and sisters all the way back in time to the beginning of our family lines. Our ancestors lived in certain ways, held different attitudes, emotional responses, attributes and health problems, which have been handed down to us through physical traits, psychic energy impingement, habituated patterns, and DNA. By healing the different negative and discordant attitudes, we transform our lives with the understanding that great healing can occur.

The other area of ancestral influence is called "impingement." This is when our ancestors whom have passed away want to do good for us or get satisfaction and/or fulfillment through us. It is important to be able to have a technique where we can do intensive healing work with ancestors so they can become healed, enlightened, and work towards their own evolution.

Like our parents care for us as helpless babies, we care for our aging helpless parents. This is a circle of life on earth. In the greater sense it is the same with the circle of our ancestors. Certain fulfillments only happen while living on earth, as do certain abilities and circumstances for growth. We are in a position on the earth to purposely help our ancestors, and in return our ancestors help us better navigate the perils and challenges of living in this time we're in.

Many of us have heard or even experienced help from ancestors who have passed over. James Van Praagh's work demonstrates that our ancestors are alive and well. However, just because they have passed over does not necessarily mean they are enlightened or more evolved than when they lived here. Regardless they are still able to be guiding influences in our lives. The more healing we give to our ancestors the more beneficial their guidance and influence to us will be.

We have heard some deceased ancestors who help their family members find houses to buy, people to marry, and business career opportunities. They have been known to save relatives from negative circumstances or relationships. Thus this reciprocation can be of the utmost benefit in obtaining the level of prosperity that gives us leisure time for our spiritual development, evolution, and realization.

We enter into this earth plane to work out karmic obscurations and when we leave, we no longer have the conditions and circumstances for such growth. Because of this we can purposefully help our ancestors in the healing process and eliminate karmic obligations. In return our ancestors healed of these conditions help us better navigate the perils and challenges we encounter here on earth.

Why is it Necessary to Work With Our Ancestors?

When our ancestors were alive, they had their own beliefs, attitudes, and desires which created its own karma. Upon death, those desires were still present, but there was no longer a means by which to fulfill them without a soul on the physical plane in a human body. When our ancestors wish to fulfill their desires through us, an energetic impingement is created. In this way, our ancestors play a part in our circumstances in life. Their traumas affect us through this energetic impingement and if these negative karmic patterns are not resolved, they are passed down through to us and our progeny. Ancestral Healing helps to clear these patterns which result in beneficial changes in our lives, positively affecting our health and well-being.

As our ancestors' karma is cleared, they become more open, free, and wise. As they heal, we heal, and so does the rest of the planet. Our relationship with our ancestors is mutually beneficial. As we pray and heal them, they in turn are more able to guide us in our earthly circumstances. Our ancestors can assist us in all aspects of fulfillment (prosperity, relationships, health, and soul evolution) not only as a means of expressing their gratitude to us, but for their own evolution.

Just as cancer, sickle-cell anemia, and diabetes are passed down through a family line, so too are problems with relationships, economic hardships, depression, anxiety, addictions, and so forth. All of us are shaped by our childhood, particularly by the interactions with, and the attitudes of the members of our immediate family. We are also influenced by the societies in which we live, the countries into which we are born, our economic strata, and the religious and cultural beliefs held by our families, and closest communities. This is a widely accepted premise within learned psychological circles. Those same family dynamics that influence and shape us on earth also exist in other realms which can profoundly affect us here on earth.

There are communities of your ancestors whose consciousness exists in the astral and other realms who lovingly watch out for you and actively guide you. Often though, the guidance provided by our ancestors can be misdirected, arising from the fog of beliefs they clung to when they lived on earth. The sometimes well-meaning, but misplaced guidance of our ancestors can be manifested in "psychic impingements," creating a collection of stumbling blocks in our lives such as frustration in realizing healthy relationships, unhappiness with one's life path and career, anger, irritation, confusion, doubt, depression, and at times severe physical symptoms.

If this karma is not resolved, it is passed on through their lineage. Ancestral healing helps clear away this karma, which results in beneficial changes to our life circumstances. As our ancestors' karma is improved, their spiritual conditions cleared and healed, so too are we and our generations to come.

Cleansing the karmic cycle of imprinted and replicated beliefs, past hurts, traumas, fears, prejudices, and other negative legacies not only allows your ancestors to provide pure assistance and unclouded help to all living relations, it also becomes a gift for you and your family. Reported benefits range widely, and are specific to each person, but many people report their lives become more synchronistic, harmonious, and loving with consideration to interpersonal relationships.

While the most profound effects will be experienced by the one seeking the healing, learning, or methodologies for spiritual growth, the effects of Ancestral Healing will also benefit siblings, cousins, one's parents, nieces, nephews, and children. In fact, depending on how far back in the bloodline the ancestor is who receives the healing; it can potentially benefit thousands upon thousands of relations, known and unknown.

Healing your ancestors can resolve physical and emotional issues and create synchronicity, but ultimately it is a powerful act of compassion, for self, family, and the world.

Ancestral Healing Ceremonies and Rituals

People in olden times generally lived in more ethically responsible times and circumstances. In small towns where everyone knows each other, there is a greater tendency for a more caring and morally aware conscience. In this way, we might say more of the people were stable and righteous. For these reasons ancestral veneration was more prevalent. But today people do not personally know each other and we are disconnected. There is leeway for more selfishness to tinge our actions and responses to others, not to mention a tendency for fear and anger, greed and hostility to taint our experiences.

Veneration of ancestors is a commonly held belief, but perhaps most specially among Asian peoples. Before the organized religions had built up their formal traditions, the practice of making offerings to ancestors was already central to the traditions of many cultures.

In many agriculture-based civilizations across the world, outside the monotheistic traditions, the dead were the focus of ancestral ceremonies and were offered food regularly. The dead ancestors were thought to be of great importance to the family, serving as intermediaries with deities, or as deities on their own. This was true in the civilizations of sub-Saharan Africa, pre-Aryan South Asia, East Asia, Mesopotamia, and the Mediterranean (Greece and Rome) as well as among Polynesian cultures.

The common belief is that ancestors uphold family tradition, help the family survive through hardships, and protect the family. Because of these roles, it is considered right and proper for the living family to remember their ancestors and make offerings to them.

As they did when they were alive, ancestors continue to provide protection, blessings, and prosperity to the family; if they are offended, usually by neglect, they may bring misfortune instead.

There are thinkers propounding the idea that formal religions have evolved from ancestor worship. The deification of ancestors as ghosts or saints has been practiced since the beginning of antiquity. This practice prevailed in many sophisticated societies such as Greece and Rome. Eventually, the belief arose among tribes and societies that their members were all descended from a common non-human ancestor—a prime ancestor which could be a god, a spirit, an animal, or a person of myth, depending on the culture and the environment in which it developed.

Ancestor veneration has a vigorous role in the complex traditions of the Chinese as well as for the people of India, Japan, Korea, Vietnam, and most parts of Southeast Asia. The many Buddhist sects in Japan such as the Nichiren and the new Shinto-oriented religions like the Tenri-ky, Moto, and Kurozumi-ky have given importance to ancestor worship. The Hoa Hao and Cao Dai traditions of Vietnam also put heavy focus on ancestor worship. Ancestor worship is performed at special places, in temples and shrines, and also at home altars.

Expressions may include rites, sacrifices, prayers, and offerings.

Though less apparent than Chinese or Japanese practices, ancestral veneration nevertheless is present among other Asian groups. For instance, the Thai's of non-Chinese descent do not have formal ancestral cults but in times of adversity, the first reaction of Thai families often is to make sacrifice and obeisance in hopes of appeasing angry ancestors. Although the majority of Filipinos are nominally Christian, they are quick to pay homage, make sacrifices, and offer prayers to their dead ancestors to court their favorable response to the needs or wishes of family members in the world of the living.

Most religions in Asia consist of a dominant component—Buddhism, Hinduism, or Islam—adulterated with various forms of animistic traditions and ancestral cult practices. Ancestral veneration is also common among African cultures, the ancient civilizations of Central and South America, including the Mayas, and the Native North American peoples.

Ancestral Healing: Gateway to Synchronicity presents an overview of the beliefs, traditions, and ceremonies on ancestral veneration in various religious and spiritual traditions while also presenting ideas as to how to use Ancestral Healing on your own, and with trained healers.

Chapter One:

African Ancestral Traditions

Ancestor veneration is quite common in African societies. Ancestor veneration complements the worship of the High God as well as minor gods and spirits. The inclusion of ancestors in the religious rites is intended to establish the strong relationship between generations past and their living descendants.

Ancestors are considered lesser spiritual beings. They serve as intermediaries between God and humans. God is considered too holy and therefore beyond direct contact by humans. The African individual thus prays to God through the ancestors, who are believed to retain great interest in the affairs of their descendants.

To deserve veneration, the ancestors should have been respected and worthy persons when alive; they should have made significant contributions to their communities which are duly acknowledged in the oral traditions. Men and women equally may be worthy of veneration.

The ancestors are believed to have power and influence on the living. They act as spiritual custodians of the community's customs and laws. They may punish offenders by bringing misfortune and ill-health. They carefully watch the conduct of the living and make them account for their deeds when they die.

Ancestor veneration is observed through prayers, offerings, and sacrifices. Prayers are entreaties addressed to ancestors for various reasons. Offerings are presentations of food and drinks, while sacrifice involves killing an animal for presentation, in order to give thanks, request for grant of petitions, ask for help to combat evil spirits, propitiate, and communicate with the ancestors. These offerings and sacrifices are tokens of fellowship, hospitality, and respect intended to strengthen the relationship among families.

One common element of ancestral rites involves the use of gall, the liquid stored in the gall bladder. Gall is used for the specific purpose of establishing contact with ancestors. It is believed that the smell and taste of gall has a special attraction for ancestors. In rituals, people singled out for ancestral contact are sprinkled with gall.

Communal veneration of ancestors is elaborate. This usually occurs at harvest times, with plenty of food and festivities. Religious rites are mixed with social functions such as public dancing, exchange of gifts, and public displays of generosity by rulers.

Ancestor veneration is a vehicle to establish and maintain cohesion in the society. The most prized possession is land, considered to be jointly owned by the ancestor and the living. Because of this, parting with land becomes an abominable act.

Ancestral veneration is also a means to regulate social relationships. Ancestors may serve as the common symbol of the town or the ruling dynasty, and therefore help preserve solidarity, and establish rulers as legitimate inheritors of authority and power.

Chapter Two:

Native/Indigenous Ancestral Traditions

In North American gathering-hunting traditions, the deceased are mourned for one year; at the end of this period, a feast is held in honor of the deceased, and prayers are said to speed them on their way, with food and tobacco and to ask them not to return. There is the inclination to avoid the corpse because it is a pollution source, thus corpses are buried, deposited in caves, or mounted on scaffolds in out-of-the way spots.

Among agricultural-hunting traditions, where the people lived in the long houses of matrilineal clans, or in homes clustered around gardens, the dead were buried in nearby spots designated for the purpose and were offered food daily. In certain traditions, notably the Wyandot, the dead were reburied in a communal pit after about twelve to sixteen years with a feast and complex rituals to mark the occasion. The tradition of holding an annual feast for the dead continues to the present.

Among gathering-hunting cultures such as the Anishnabe, especially those that possess a wood stove, a small amount of food is taken from daily meals, put in the fire of the stove, and offered to the world of the spirits—Sky, Earth, the Four

Directions, and special spirits. Among agricultural-hunting traditions, the offering is also addressed to the spirit realm but, in addition, the dead of the clan are included.

In the cultures of Polynesia, sub-Saharan Africa, South and East Asia, and the Mediterranean, mediumism (spirit possession) was a central aspect of ancestral rituals. They believed that the dead, beginning with the dead of the family, and then the other clan dead, who have become deities, would possess particular individuals in order that the family, the clan, or the community interact and commune with the realm of the spirits.

Mediumism was not as widespread among the Native American traditions. The possible exception may have been the Inca of the Andes, where the ruling married couple represented the Sun and the Moon. On the death of the male ruler, his corpse was mummified and placed in the temple to the Sun; upon the death of the female ruler, her mummified corpse was deposited in the temple to the Moon. Food and other offerings were given to the mummies daily, and they were consulted for advice on important matters when needed. However, no spirit possession was involved.

In the cultures of the Northwest Coast, ancestors are important for various reasons such as the belief that a deity served as the ancestor who originated the clan.

In the Kwakwaka'wakw culture, the originating clan ancestor was believed to have fallen from the sky or emerged from the sea, turned human, and started the clan. These sacred ancestors were present as masked dancers during potlatch ceremonies.

Among the Tlingit, a memorial potlatch ceremony was performed when a person died. Gifts were symbolically presented to the guests, but since it was believed that the clan's matrilineal ancestors were also present, the gifts were really intended for the ancestors.

The ancestors are also deemed present when masks (and other dance paraphernalia), handed down from earlier generations, are worn by the living clan members. As they perform the dance, they are transformed into the clan ancestors who are then present in the ceremony to welcome the newly-dead into the spiritual world of the clan dead.

In the Pueblo traditions of the Southwest, such as the Hopi, the ceremonies of winter are the occasion for their deities, the Katsina, to enter the communities. Their presence in the village is manifested in the masked dancers who are not possessed by these spirits, but are actually transformed and become the Katsina. Strictly speaking, the Katsina are not ancestors, but they invoke clan memory of their matrilineal ancestors. The Katsina are believed to live in the realm where the Sun goes to after sunset—which is also the realm of the dead. Their appearance in the Hopi villages thus connotes a visit by the dead in general, but not individually.

The realm of the dead is thought to be a watery underworld, and the dead are thus perceived to exert influence over rain, which makes agriculture in the arid semidesert region possible. When the Hopi pray for the life-giving rain to come, their prayers are thus directed to both Katsina and the clan ancestors.

In the Native American traditions, therefore, the dead members of the family and the clan are recognized to be spiritually potent but are not deities. They manifest their presence in the transformed masked dancers but they do not take over the bodies of—that is, the spirits do not possess—the dancers. The living can reach these ancestors through prayer and rituals, and the ancestors may appear to them in dreams. Ancestors can influence the fortunes of the living but only in subtle ways.

In the ancient civilization of the Maya, belief in the influence of ancestors and in reincarnation played central roles in their customs, which persist to the present. Ancestors deemed semi-divine, probably because of the power and influence they wielded in their lifetimes, were reborn as gods and worked for the benefit of their descendants—but only if the descendants properly observed the rituals of ancestor worship. These ancestral ceremonies were held in temples atop their tombs.

Tombs or shrines served two important purposes; they provided access to the spirit world and legitimacy to inheritance and lineage. They were declarations that the lineage belonged to the clan since the time of its sacred founders. The oral traditions on lineage could trace back hundreds of years of descent with specific details about names and marriages. The land was therefore theirs, and it was inherited from the gods, the clan's sacred founders.

ANCESTOR BELIEFS IN HAWAIIAN RELIGIOUS TRADITIONS

Ancestor worship was also a central part of Hawaiian practices, and many of their rituals involved the propitiation of gods, ancestors, or spirit guardians. As in other cultures, death rituals differed for common people and for chiefs and other leaders. Common people death rituals were simple affairs, and their remains were likely to be buried in sand dunes and similar separate areas. Death rituals for chiefs were more elaborate, and their remains were placed inside caves along with ceremonial canoes and other burial offerings.

The Hawaiians call their ancestral gods or guardian spirits the Aumakua. Not all ancestors become aumakua; the aumakua are spirits selected from among the dead because of high achievements and/or special qualities demonstrated during their lifetime. They are deified after death and eventually become gods. Both male and female ancestors become aumakua, and they may appear in animal, plant or mineral form. Just as family members share common ancestors, they also share common aumakua—who establish a spiritual bond that joins all family members.

The aumakua perform diverse functions. They serve as messengers conveying prayers and petitions from the living to the akua, who are the more powerful—but more distant—gods.

The aumakua are always in circulation around the living family members, making daily communication with them possible. They bring gifts from the spirit world to the world of the living, including dreams at night, visions, and healing. The aumakua were believed to be the spirits the living could consult for help with their problems. They provided a link to ancestral roots.

In Hawaiian society, the family was the dominant social unit. In this context, the relationship between the living family members and aumakua, who were beloved family guardians, was intimate. The aumakua were associated with important social values and, since Hawaiians viewed salvation as a family rather than an individual affair, the aumakua had a significant influence on a living person's future journey in the afterlife. Traditionally, the aumakua were asked for advice in making important decisions and to participate in rituals and ceremonies—such as the ho'oponopono process, the naming of children, and the welcoming of a dying family member into the realm of the dead. There may also be animal aumakua, to represent the family's ancestral connections to that species or to a god (akua) represented by one or more animals or elements.

The relationship is a close partnership. The aumakua give protection to the family and community, warning of dangers, counsel, healing, forgiveness, retribution, discipline, and order to the family; in return, the ohana do good deeds, heed their warnings, propitiate and offer sacrifice to the aumakua, offer food and nourishment, and pay homage to them.

The specific steps by which an ancestor turns into aumakua are obscure, but the living members of the family and the community (ohana) were important parts of the process. When a chief died, the body was laid before the multitude so that it could be deified and, through a series of elaborate ceremonies, transformed into an aumakua. This solemn ritual, called kaku'ai lasted ten days or more. Towards the end of the ritual, the priest (kahuna) recited special incantations which imparted godlike power to the bones of the deceased (in earlier stages, the flesh had been stripped from the corpse). The dead chief was then worshipped as a real god.

The family of ordinary people went through a similar kaku'ai ritual for their deceased relatives. Once the flesh was gone from the corpse, they would wrap the bones in red and black tapa and take them to a volcano. After some ceremonies and ritual incantations were performed by the kahuna, the bones were thrown into the volcano.

It is the living, and especially the kahuna, who deify the dead. The participation of the priest is essential as he performs the prayers, incantations, sacrifices, symbols, and all other requirements for the ritual. While death conferred immortality on everyone, only a few people were eligible to ascend to aumakua status. It was an honor given as a result of strength of character, potent mana, and service to the ohana demonstrated during life. Whatever these criteria the basic idea is that if he or she was good enough in life to be honored by the community, he or she would be good enough to be revered in the afterlife as a protecting spirit of the family.

Chapter Three:

FAR EAST ANCESTRAL TRADITIONS

In Hindu beliefs, the spirit of the dead (sonum) undergoes a series of stages after death that progressively transforms them from being potentially dangerous to the living at the start to being benign and detached from the living at the end. The Hindu traditions distinguish between the recently dead (bhuta or preta), who can pose problems to the family or community, and those dead for a longer time (pitr), who are considered harmless.

In the first stages, the sonums dwell in certain features of the local environment associated with the manner in which they died. For example, the sonum of a person killed by a leopard is believed to inhabit termite mounds, whereas other forms of death may make sonums occupy other locations in the local environment such as a path, a clearing, a body of water, or a rock. The location of a sonum is designated by tradition.

In the early stages, the belief is that sonums want to bring death upon other people in the community in the same manner by which they died. As time passes and through appropriate ancestral ceremonies, the problematic dead can be transformed into ancestors.

Before they become ancestors, sonums go to areas farther from the village and dwell in locations in the wilderness. The degree of danger posed by the dead can thus be predicted by the location of the sonum and their proximity to the living.

Ancestors dwell in the underworld traditionally identified within the village or in cultivated fields and pools that belong to their family. Once they become ancestors, the sonums are less dangerous although they can still inflict harm such as drought, disease, or infertility if angered. They may demand rituals and offerings on a regular basis and can become easily displeased if they are neglected. Appropriately propitiated with ritual offerings, the ancestors can benefit the living by bringing fertility to the crops, wealth and good fortune to the family members.

Ancestors are perceived to sometimes be on a level with the high gods, although they are only of a semi-divine status. The place of the ancestors is separate from the earthly realm of living humans (bhuloka), from the abode of other kinds of spirits (antariksa), and from the exalted heaven of the high gods (svarga). It is only after the first anniversary of death when the dead are elevated to the semi-divine level.

The term pitr is singular, which means father; in the plural pitarah, it means forefathers, forebears, and great-grandfathers. Father and forefather are thus ritually perceived to be on the same level with the son.

The dead stay as ancestors for only three generations, after which they move to a greater collectivity, de-individualized, and worshipped as a group (called visve devah, which literally means "all gods"). The three generations progressively rise in status but decrease in proximity to the living. Each new death brings the deceased a notch closer to heaven. Thus it is said "a man wins worlds through a son, gains eternity through a grandson, but reaches heaven through the grandson of his son." This underlines the importance of sons in the salvation of a man's soul. The son (putra) is thus seen as one who saves his father from hell. After this stay among the ancestors, the spirit may be reborn in this world or, if completely purified, will join the gods in heaven.

Through rituals and ceremonies, the living members continuously reestablish the relationship of gods and ancestors. The two groups are considered deities (devata) but the ancestor rituals performed in their honor have distinct differences. For example, when calling upon the gods, the sacred thread is worn on the left shoulder; when calling upon ancestors, the thread is on the right shoulder. Even numbers are used when dealing with gods and odd numbers with ancestors. Gods are offered barley or rice grains, but ancestors get sesame seeds. The person in charge of the sacrifice looks east when performing it for the gods and south when doing it for ancestors. The sacrificial place for gods is shaped as a square, but is round for ancestors.

When a Hindu dies, the body is cremated (as a sacrifice to the fire agni) or may be brought to the nearest riverside for burial. The spirit of the newly deceased (more precisely known as preta) is ritually given an invisible temporary body using pindas (balls of cooked rice and sesame) over a period of ten days. Sacred texts (usually from the Bhagavad Gita or the Garuda Purana) are read at the house during the transition period, while at the riverside the funerary Brahmans perform the special rituals that create the invisible spiritual body (ativahika). During the ten-day period, the head is ritually created first and the digestive powers last; the period also corresponds to the ten lunar months associated with the human gestation period and to the ten days of special rites held at the delivery room to purify an infant after birth. After this period, the preta is appropriately covered and ready for the passage.

Over the next 12 months, daily offerings and sacrifices and special monthly rites every day of the new moon are done. On the first death anniversary, a funerary Brahman or a family priest may recite mantras related to the ancestry of the deceased. In a rite called sapindikarana, the pinda for the deceased is blended with three others symbolizing the nearest three generations of ancestors (father, grandfather, and great-grandfather). There is also a ritual obeisance to ancestral generations older than the great-grandfather, who may be poised to be reincarnated in this world or to ascend to the higher reaches of heaven.

Ancestor Beliefs in Japanese Religious Traditions

The religious syncretism of Japanese traditions should always be kept in mind. It is often difficult to distinguish whether the origins of a given concept or deity are Shinto, Buddhist, Confucian, or Daoist. But while these elements have blended quite thoroughly, there are many instances where the ordinary Japanese can draw a clear demarcation between, for example, Shinto and Buddhist practices.

A prime example is the common practice of marking, after a suitable period has elapsed since death occurred, the change of status of a dead relative from a buddha to a god, or kami. This change of status is usually said to happen on the final memorial service for the individual soul, which marks the end of a long process of purification of the soul. At this time, the memorial tablet deposited in the Buddhist altar of the Shinto shrine in the community is removed. For most ordinary people, this occasion usually occurs on the thirty-third (sometimes on the fiftieth) anniversary of death; for Shinto priests, this may occur much sooner on the sixth or thirteenth anniversary.

Regardless of religious origin, the death of a person triggers a series of rites and ceremonies that ultimately culminate in the final memorial service held thirty-three (or fifty) years after death. The Japanese believe that during the period between the occurrence of death and the final memorial service, the person's spirit undergoes ritual and symbolic purification. The spirit gradually moves from the stage of having close association with the corpse, which is perceived as being both polluting and dangerous, to the stage of being purified and benign, thus losing its individual identity, and finally entering the domain of generalized ancestral spirits.

The process of transformation has been described by Herman Ooms in the following way: *The ancestor cult creates order in the passing of time as experienced in the household. It gives order to the inevitable fact of death and by the same token orders of life; everybody is destined to become an ancestor. The order is structured as a process where the stages leading to this final purpose of life are outlined (memorial services, steps on the path of ancestorhood). Everybody finds himself in due time on the appropriate stage. The shift from one stage to the next and the acquisition of this new status are not the result of individual endeavor or personal achievement of the subject himself. The outsiders have certain power over him, because it is thanks to their loyalty that one can become an ancestor. But their power of intervention is limited; the order is fixed and only when the time is ripe will the change occur almost as the result of a natural growth.*

The living family members can help the dead spirit become an ancestor, through their loyalty and the ceremonies they perform. The noteworthy feature of these ceremonies for the dead is that from the time of death until the final service, it is the household and its members who assume primary responsibility for their performance.

It is normal that as the years pass since a person's death, it is quite likely that no one else save the household members will look after his or her spirit. Many people will probably attend the funeral; but fewer will be around for the rites held on the forty-ninth day; and their number will get progressively less with each passing year as memorial services are held.

Even the Shinto priest will progressively have less involvement in the ceremonies for the deceased over the years. Thus, it can truly be said that, by their observance of the various rites, it is only the household members who can prevent their departed relatives from turning into wandering spirits and becoming worthy ancestors instead.

In particular rites, all household members may need to be involved; in others, only the head of the household and the wife; and in a few others, any individual who desires to propitiate the ancestors may perform the rites.

During funerals, the priest's role is confined to reciting sutras. The principal actors are the household members: they light the incense, carry the memorial tablet in the procession, and gather the bones and ashes after cremation. The household members also officiate during the memorial services which are normally held at the household altar.

The household altar contains memorial tablets for the household's ancestors (who are defined as the ascending generations of the head of the house and his wife); it may have tablets for family members who were regular residents of the house before they died, and for children (of past heads of the house) who never married. It may also contain tablets for people who are not at all ancestors of the current household members.

The tablets are there primarily because of a fundamental belief that each deceased person should be cared for and because the Japanese want to guard against the danger posed by wandering spirits. It is crucial that each spirit have a place, i.e. be settled and located somewhere, because wandering spirits can pose a threat to the living if they are left uncared for and abandoned.

In the 49-day period immediately following death, the rites have the objective of separating or severing the close association of the corpse with the spirit of the person and to liberate it from attachment to the world of the living.

To accomplish these objectives, the household members attempt to confuse the spirit. Before taking the coffin outside the house for the funeral procession, the pallbearers carry it in circles around the room where the wake was held. The path followed by the procession is usually swept clean, in order to erase the mourners' footprints and to prevent the spirit from finding its way back to the house. The mourners take a different route when they return from the cemetery. The funeral service highlights a symbolic separation of the spirit from the corpse or ashes: a memorial tablet (which represents the spirit) is removed and taken to the household altar, where it becomes the object of veneration for the first 49 days.

The transfer of the memorial tablet to the house after the funeral may seem to contradict the steps taken to confuse the spirit before the funeral. Relatives often do this because they do not want the spirit to return to the wrong house; once the spirit has been separated from the corpse at the end of the funeral services, the act of carrying the temporary memorial tablet directly to the deceased's former house ensures that the spirit is properly settled in the place where all ceremonies in its honor will be held.

Subsequently, a series of rites is then conducted, with the primary intention of helping the spirit of the newly dead (shirei) to be transformed into an ancestral spirit (sorei). A low table is set up in front of but not inside the altar, and a temporary tablet, a photograph of the dead relative, several candles, incense, an incense burner, and a small gong (or bell) are placed on the table. On the forty-ninth day usually, but sometimes on the third death anniversary, the temporary tablet and the photograph are removed. A permanent memorial tablet, bearing the posthumous name of the deceased, is placed inside the altar along with other tablets.

On the first bon festival (a festival for the dead), the new memorial tablet is separated from the older ones and accorded special treatment. It is placed on a separate altar in the main room of the house and more elaborate offerings are made to it than to the older tablets. The separation is intended to prevent the spirit of the newly dead from contaminating the more purified souls of the long dead.

In the ensuing years, successive memorial rites are held, and the dead person becomes more distant and memories of him or her gradually fade. On the final memorial service, the individual's spirit leaves the ranks of the household dead and passes into a larger collectivity, the realm of the ancestral spirits, who can confer positive benefits upon mankind through their supernatural power or, if neglected, can inflict distress and sickness.

Ancestor Beliefs in Chinese Religious Traditions

Chinese ancestor worship puts emphasis on the belief that the spirits of dead relatives inhabit a spiritual realm entirely separate from the world of the living but that, despite the separation, the relationship between the inhabitants of both realms is not entirely severed.

The corpse itself is considered a source of pollution. But through the observance of rituals and ceremonies, the spirit can be transformed into a beneficent force. After the corpse is buried, the Chinese believe that elements of the dead person's spirit remain and need to be nurtured by the relatives and descendants. If they are suitably cared for by the descendants, ancestors can help bring wealth, good fortune, and many sons. If neglected, the spirits of the deceased can turn malevolent and bring misfortune on the family and community.

Originally, ancestor ceremonies were reserved only for a privileged few, particularly the rulers of a kingdom and the hereditary elite. There were strict regulations that distinguished the observances of rulers from those of state officials, and those of officials from the ordinary people's observances. The building of ancestor temples was forbidden to common people, as were making offerings to ancestors belonging to generations older than their grandparents. Official regulations also imposed rules on the number of ancestors entitled to ceremonies, the timing of sacrifices, and other details.

Ancestor rituals were performed at household altars. These involved daily presentations of food and incense by household members. Ritual observances were more frequent and more personalized; in addition to the traditional spirit tablet, an image was used (eventually supplanted by photographs). The deceased became ancestors only after a sufficient period of mourning elapsed.

Every new ancestor was considered the family protector. As each new generation died, the power of the ancestor would weaken. After three generations, all power would be gone and sacrifices would no longer be made. However, clan founders and those members who achieved status in their lifetimes did not lose power.

It was believed that the male ancestors of the patriarch-based lineage were sources of symbolic capital. For common folk, the power from their ancestors was zealously guarded by the descendants. The more powerful a person was while living, the more powerful his spirit was believed to be in the spiritual realm. From about 1600 B.C., the spirits of imperial ancestors were considered sources of sacred power to be harnessed only by the ruler. As ruling dynasties replaced previous dynasties, they incorporated the ancestors of the earlier ruling houses, and various theories were made to explain how ancestors of a different, older dynasty could become ancestors of the new, unrelated dynasty.

Belief in the potentially beneficent power of ancestors existed among the Chinese long before the advent of Confucian thought. Confucianism eventually remolded these beliefs after it was adopted as the state doctrine in the second century B.C. To replace the notion of reciprocity between the living family members and the departed ancestors, Confucianism stressed the concept of filial piety or the duty children owed to their parents.

Confucius is said to have defined filial piety this way: "That parents, while alive, should be served according to li; that, when dead, they should be buried according to li; and that offerings should be made according to li." The term li can mean both "ritual" and "proper behavior" and has always had a religious dimension to it. Confucianism contains detailed procedures for how ancestor ceremonies should be performed and provides the rationale for the rites.

Chapter Four:

Western Ancestral Traditions

As many of us are more familiar with the traditional religions of modern day, we can also look to them for examples of what we already know about ancestral healing and its effect on our lives.

Ancestor Beliefs in Jewish Religious Traditions

The Jewish people have suffered because of their faith. Since long before the days of Moses, they have been persecuted.

As a result, they have become a faith founded on the idea of a strong connection to their ancestors. Jews focus worship on the idea of one God, a God who takes care of them, but ancestors have a special place as well. Ancestors are the ones who brought the current generation into the world and as a result are given respect and gratitude.

The same respect, which is reserved for God, is given to the relatives of Jews, as they are often just as important.

According to the Hebrew faith, the soul or the nefesh, (sometimes known as the ruah or the spirit) is contained within the body and can also be inhabited for short periods of time by other beings.

The dead were treated with utmost care and respect. Bodies were completely buried in Israelite times, though later on, they were burned, as the dead were considered especially holy. When the body was burned, the soul was completely released from the body and able to find rest.

Gifts were given and the bodies of some ancestors were buried at the homes of their relatives to keep them close.

Men were supposed to keep a fire alive in the hearth to demonstrate continued worship for family ancestors.

The soul is thought by Jewish practitioners to leave after death, but the spirit lives on. In modern times, the body is not burned, but it is given the same respect. It is not embalmed and is buried soon after death, preferably by placing the body directly into the ground. The body should not have an autopsy and organ donation is forbidden except in extreme circumstances. The body should remain complete and pure as it enters the ground.

However, anthropologists now believe that ancestors may not have been as venerated as once thought since there is no evidence of special names for deceased ancestors, and it is thought these names would be necessary for worship.

The shiva is a period of mourning that takes place after a Jew has died. This is a strict period in which the mourners gather at the house around the body and talk about the person who has passed. There is no bathing, changing of clothes, or eating. All daily activities cease in order to show reverence and respect.

Lineage is marked upon the gravestones of the deceased again to show reverence to the ancestry of those in the Jewish family.

The adherence to the past via the Torah allows one to speculate that the Jewish people believe strongly in worshiping their ancestors through the practice of tradition.

From holidays such as Passover, in which a plague passed over the homes of the Jews, to the New Year or Rosh Hashanah, these old traditions continue into the modern day, allowing the connection to the past to live on.

ANCESTOR BELIEFS IN CHRISTIAN RELIGIOUS TRADITIONS

It's no surprise that the Christian faith takes its reverence of ancestors quite seriously. In the Old Testament (Leviticus 26:45), a reader can see a long list of genealogies detailing ancient Christian lineage.

Genesis also includes a long list of the path of man to God, again, demonstrating in detail how the ancestors were not only revered, but also worshiped through special placement in the Bible alongside the parables and the teachings of God himself.

It is also interesting to note the descriptions of ancestral lines in the Bible were not necessarily seen necessarily as God-like. Instead, they were seen as humans and fallible. This allowed those who read about these people to see themselves in the actions these characters took.

These humans were the Chosen Ones, and that's why they were mentioned. God chose them for special purposes—and therefore, they should be looked up to.

However, it should be no surprise that revering the ancestors as anything like God would not be permissible. Since God is the only deity to be worshiped, even ancestors must play a minor role both in and out of church.

In times of death, the deceased are not worshiped so much as they are acknowledged for living God's purpose for him while on earth during their life time.

However, it is also seen that when a person does go to heaven, they rejoin their heavenly family. Some believe the holy family—God, Jesus, Mary, etc.—to be their own family. As a result, some might keep statues of these figures in their homes or they might have pieces of jewelry with their images or with the images of the saints.

Since all of these people have come from God and seek to be a part of God's plan, they are all our ancestors. Humans, coming from the original couple of Adam and Eve, are descended from the people who God created in his own image. And as a result, though the human race may have been banished from the Garden of Eden, Christians often look to this first couple, not for worship, but for the reminder that they are fallible–only God is a point of worship and of praise.

Ancestor Beliefs in Islamic Religious Traditions

Sufism is thought to be the inner practice of Islam, more mystical in nature than the more modern experience.

Within the practice of Sufism, one has to find a teacher to learn the tenets as handed down by Muhammad. These tenets cannot be taught in a book, but rather need to be taught by a direct teacher.

One must live with their spiritual teacher for an extended period of time, helping to serve others—tending to the needy, performing community services, etc.

Through these teachings, the student learns that only God matters and only God is where their focus should be. As a result ancestor worship does not become a focal point of the teachings, though Muhammad is obviously revered for his part in the process of obtaining the information for the Koran (Qur'an).

In order to recognize themselves, a practitioner of Sufism needs to renounce all else in his or her life and focus only on their connection with God. This means they might turn away from family members and from any past that does not include Sufism.

The whirling dervishes are an example of one way Sufi practitioners show their complete and utter devotion to God. By whirling around in circles, they practice the art of dancing in order to symbolize man's journey from their imperfect life to a state of perfection in finding God and his goodness.

Chapter Five:

New Age Ancestral Communication

Ancestral practices evolved around the crucial concepts of death and life after death. Death is the last turning point every human being must confront. What happens after death is a mystery, and it is difficult to contemplate that after so much trouble and resources used to create human life, all these would suddenly go to waste due to death.

This may explain why there is a pervasive belief across cultures in the immortality of the soul, and the corollary belief of social interaction between the inhabitants of the physical and the spiritual realms, the living and the dead. These ancestral beliefs have helped develop the ceremonies and rituals of ancestral cults. Death brings an end to normal social interaction between living beings, but memories of the deceased ancestors continue. The desire to re-establish social interaction is normal for those who hold these beliefs. This desire can be expected among the living and, presumably, among the dead.

This interaction can be reactivated through communication with the ancestral spirits through psychic mediums. The New Age traditions, which seek to achieve a fuller integration of the individual with the environment, nature, and the spiritual realms, encourage the creation of active communication channels between the living and the dead.

But while humans may all have the potentiality to communicate with the spirits of their ancestors, some individuals are more adept at this than others, some individuals are more articulate in the language of the spirits than others, and some individuals are more able to enter or leave the altered states of consciousness necessary to establish the communications link. It is these individuals who are best able to perform the functions of psychic mediumship.

One of the better known psychic mediums in the New Age traditions is James Van Praagh, who describes himself as a "survival evidence medium." Mediums can help individuals gain proof that life does exist after death, removing one of the veils that hide the mystery of death. Communication with the spirits can be one such proof. Van Praagh explains this is done telepathically, i.e. mind-to-mind communication or, more accurately, spirit-to-spirit communication.

The telepathic thought received by the medium may carry along with it the personality of an ancestor. If the person was very emotional in his or her life, the telepathic thought may be laden with emotional feeling. If the person was more cerebral, the telepathic thought will convey that same personality from the spirit world.

Mediums say the most common idea the spirits want the living to understand is that they are alive, that they have seen up close both the good and the bad things they did in their lives, and that they want the living to know they love them and are with them.

In the modern world, people have become separated from the ceremonies and rituals once held to show respect for and to commune with their ancestors. Households and clans used to be the focal point of ancestor worship, but in most societies today these social units are disappearing while the smaller conjugal family has replaced them as the basic social unit.

Our traditional channels for communing and communicating with ancestors are disappearing. We need to revisit ancestral ceremonies and establish new channels of communication, as well as ways to actively advance those loved-ones who have departed.

As you now know ancestors can be a great help to us, but can also be a hindrance to our fulfillment in life. In ancestral healing, the ancestors are contacted and healed of their different misunderstandings and discordant, negative attitudes, and unfulfilled desires. Our ancestors have no way of clearing their karma while they are awaiting rebirth, but as you seek healing they benefit as well.

It is important to be able to have a technique where we can do intensive healing work with our ancestors so they can become healed, enlightened, and work towards their own evolution. Certain fulfillments can only happen while living on the earth, and certain abilities and circumstances for growth. So we are in a position while on earth to purposefully help our ancestors, and in return our ancestors can help us navigate the perils and challenges of living on earth.

Chapter Six:

Stories of Ancestral Healing

After 35 years of devoted spiritual practice, instruction, and lifestyle, Joseph is aware of his own spiritual connections as well as of the connections we all share with each other and our ancestors. Not only does he conduct Ancestral Healing sessions, but he also teaches these esoteric yogic practices and methods, so that anyone of sincere commitment can heal their entire bloodline—past, present, and future.

Why would you want to receive or learn this art? Ancestral Healing purifies and clears the reciprocity of the relationship between the living and their ancestors who wish to benefit their kin. The healing that takes place with your ancestors through Joseph, and the yogic arts he teaches, is an aspect of healing which is not normally available to them. This is a great gift that cleanses this connection of reciprocity, so that ancestors can give pure help to all living family members.

Another aspect of this work is that, when an ancestor is healed, that healing will be felt throughout the entire bloodline; mostly through the one who seeks the healing, but also through their siblings and cousins, parents, nieces and nephews and all who follow. Depending on how far back in the bloodline the ancestor is who receives this gift, the healing can potentially affect thousands upon thousands of relatives.

Truly, healing your ancestors is an act of great compassion for self, family, and the world.

Client Karl Kopitske writes the following about his experiences with ancestral healing:

> We like to think positively of the gifts our ancestors have given us. You might have your father's jaw line or your mother's eyes, your grandfather's talent on the piano or your grandmother's love of dance. As we move from genealogy to genetics, our doctors warn us to be aware of negative family patterns of disease. Your physician might ask you if there is a history of diabetes in your family. We inherit propensities for illness as well as health through our DNA, but what if there were a way to clear the negative influences of our ancestors?

This is what a client known as 'Frank' had to say about his experiences with Joseph in a letter to friends and colleagues:

> "I was blessed to spend several days with [Joseph]. I believe everyone should take advantage of this awesome opportunity to experience profound healing in a way that you might never have before. And I wanted to let you know about his work and how it powerfully impacted my life so you can see where that belief comes from.
>
> Ancestral Healing was not at all what I thought it would be. To be honest I was dubious. I thought it would be a feel-good meditation experience and then we would go along our merry way.
>
> For starters, Ancestral Healing is like a cross between being in the

presence of a really good medium and experiencing a deep healing that is immediately apparent but takes days to really understand as it continues to unfold. As he explained it, Joseph is healing the influences our ancestors have on us even today. It took me a bit to wrap my head around that, but as I went through the process I understood what he meant.

Joseph began working with me by asking about my mother's side. He asked what was wrong with the right side of my mother's head and then why she couldn't hear. He had no idea that she is deaf on that side (few people know that, in fact).

He then asked about my mother's mother and the women in the two prior generations. He said they all had very disapproving looks on their faces and were wagging their fingers. Again, totally spot on. My grandmother and her mother were very disapproving women. This fact had a huge impact on my mother's life and on mine as well. Disapproval is something that has always been scary for me.

Joseph made some hand gestures and told me those issues were healed. And they have been. I'm moving through my life with much more confidence. But that was only the beginning.

After working with my mother's side, he moved over to my father's side. My father passed away back in 2001. Joseph nailed my dad's personal issues immediately. He said my father was terrified of failing. And that he felt like he never really succeeded in life. Not only is that true, these are the biggest issues I have been facing for the last couple of years. I've been afraid that I wouldn't ever be able to do better than my father-- that anything I attempted to do would inevitably fail. That is gone. Really gone.

If we had just stopped at those two issues, that would have been plenty. But we went even further. I was able to communicate with my great-grandfather about a question I've always had about his life. I was surprised at the response I got, but it was consistent with what my Aunt Dorothy always said about him.

I was set free from an overly romantic vision I had about his life. This is something I had started believing when I was a teenager. And I realized, after working with Joseph, that I had been competing with my great-grandfather to be even more of a pioneer than he was.

Since Joseph was here, I feel like I've been set free. Making decisions based on what is right for me (as opposed to the influences coming from the past) has been easy and natural.

Before I was always afraid I would be met by disapproval. Gone!

And that everything I attempted to do would fail. Also gone! It all happened in a much shorter time than I thought would be possible.

Much love, Frank

The success stories from past clients are numerous:

"When I did the Ancestral Healing Workshop we had the Luminaries in our ancestral lineage to work with. Probably what was a most significant point was that several months after the Workshop my Mother actually had told me verbally, for the first time that I know or can remember, is that she loved me. That was out of the

clear blue at the end of a conversation. So I thought, this must really work! The relationship with her has continued to improve tremendously! The ancestral work that I have done with Joseph has just been phenomenal. Through the work my daughter, who is bipolar, has been able to decrease her medications. It's a miracle! Another miracle is the fact that I am speaking to my parents and that I have moved out of judgment and can see them with a little compassion, I think is huge. I have also participated in a few Distance Healings. It was right when I had been in deep depression and I was coming out of it. The last one I did I went into meditation at the scheduled time of the healing. What I noticed is that when I was in the meditation I really felt like I wasn't even there. It seemed like it was a lot of time that passed, but it wasn't a lot of time at all. I was just gone and it was really very nice. Whatever was left of the depression lifted, I am so much better now."
Jeanmarie Reynolds / Psychotherapist / St. Louis, Missouri

"My greatest benefit was during one of the group sessions where I had hands on healing. About six months prior to coming to Joseph I had been to several different cardiologists and determined I had dilated cardiomyopathy, a condition in which the ejection fraction (rate of blood going through the heart due to a damaged heart muscle) was very, very low. My family physician was hosting Joseph one night at his office with other patients of his attending; I remember when Joseph was working on my heart. I definitely felt something was happening. There was what seemed like warmth in my chest, then a pain and then tightness and then more pain. Then I started having quickness of breath. Then I was caught up in the whole experience of wondering was I having a heart attack? I realized I was in the presence of a doctor, in a doctor's office and I realized no I wouldn't be having a heart attack from what had just happened. So I realized in my conscious mind that it's okay, don't worry it's just whatever Joseph could do or provide... it happened. The healing happened at that one time. A month later I went to see another cardiologist and I received a more positive evaluation. I went through a battery of tests, echocardiogram and other tests and he said that my ejection fraction is just a small amount less than normal for someone my age.

I said," How can that be?"

He said, "Well this is what the test shows."

I said, "Do you have the paper work that shows what the last test was?"

He said it was a remarkable improvement. I told the doctor that the only thing that's happened to me is that I was on a new drug.

I said," In that short period of time would the drug have made such a change or improvement in my heart's ability to pump?"

He said that the drug would not have changed my heart that much in that short a period of time. I had seen three cardiologists and this one specialist seemed to be very open-minded. He came highly recommended and was one of the directors at a noted hospital in Downtown Chicago. I told him about the experience with Joseph. And I said, "Do you think this hands-on healing made this improvement possible and have you ever experienced this?"

He thought it was possible and I was fortunate that I was able to receive healing other than traditional drug therapy or surgery. I really experienced some profound healing that was documented. I know I must always remain grateful. I experienced a miracle!"

Jonathan Shook / Sales, Boat Builder, Artist / Rocky Point, North Carolina

Chapter Seven: Ancestral Ceremonies and Rituals

The very same family dynamics that influence and shape us here on earth exist in other realms, which also profoundly influence us here on earth. This concept bears repeating: There are communities of your ancestors whose consciousness exists in the astral and other realms, who lovingly watch out for you and actively guide you. Yes, Virginia, the spirit of your great grandfather, the one that held such high morals (including being an active member of the KKK), sincerely believes he is serving your highest good when he puts energetic blocks between you and that beautiful African-American man you feel so drawn towards.

Just like Romeo and Juliet, the limiting belief systems that exist within our families, the feuds, fears, inhibitions, prejudices, and credos, echo around us from the well meaning but sometimes misplaced guidance of the spirits of our ancestors. These attentions can manifest as psychic impingements and stumbling blocks in our lives, resulting in things like being in the wrong place at the wrong time, frustration in realizing healthy relationships, unhappiness with one's life path and career, anger, irritation, doubt, confusion, general restlessness, and other inhibiting or even severe symptoms, including purely physical ones.

Our ancestors bequeath a lot to us, through our genetic material, cultural traditions, emotional patterns, and developmental opportunities. And as multi-dimensional beings in the same big soup together, our ancestors continue to exert their influence, but can only guide us through the cloud of beliefs they clung to when they left the earth. Obviously, there are many areas where, because of social change, what worked for our forbearers in their day won't work for us today.

So what can be done to heal our ancestors now, in the present moment? Since they are going to affect us one way or the other, how can we help our ancestors attain clarity so that their guidance comes to us from the wisest place, and they can have the most beneficial effect upon our lives?

CREATING ANCESTRAL CONNECTIONS

While it might seem as though we are very far from our ancestors in our daily lives, this is far from the case. There are many opportunities for us to reconnect with our ancestors in respectful and healing ways.

By taking the time to connect with our ancestors, we begin to heal the wounds of the past and create a stronger connection between ourselves and our futures.

Though thinking about our ancestors helps to keep their spirits alive, taking a more active role will allow you to connect with your past in a more visceral and often more meaningful way.

We feel we are doing more when we are actually doing, rather than simply thinking about what we can do.

Here are some ideas for ways you can begin to create ancestral connections and benefit your ancestors in your own life and practices:

CEREMONIES

Ceremonies are special events in which we can commemorate our ancestors in a loving and supportive way in our own lives. Ceremonies do not have to be complicated, but they can be quite powerful in terms of creating a link between the past and our present.

An example of a ceremony you can do is one practiced on the Day of the Dead – or El Dia De Los Muertos. This is also known as All Saints Day in many Christian denominations.

On this day, the dead are celebrated in various ways. One might create a ceremony in which the dead are remembered in prose or in a lively ceremony in which songs are sung and dances are performed. The dead are given a voice to exist in the world once again.

Some ceremonies include time in which the participants might try to speak with the dead in some way. Often the Day of the Dead and Halloween are thought to be days when the veil between the two worlds—the dead and the living—is the thinnest. Often, divination is done on these days to help the living contact the dead and send their love or receive messages.

PRAYERS

No matter what faith you might practice or what deities you believe in, we can all understand the idea of prayer.

Prayer can be as simple as taking a moment or two to release your wishes and your desires into the universe. This can be a completely private moment or you might wish to share your prayers with others in your faith group.

Prayers can be simply conversations with your ancestors, or times when you ask for support or guidance from the past. You might feel things in response to your prayers or you might notice changes in your life long after the prayer has been said.

You can offer prayers to your ancestors in a sacred space or you might want to simply pray to your ancestors whenever the time seems right and appropriate. Some people like to offer prayers on certain anniversaries or they might want to offer prayers during times of their own confusion and distress.

What you need to know now is that there is no 'bad' time to pray—your ancestors are always listening.

Another way to use prayer for the benefit of your ancestors is to pray that God bless them with purification, forgiveness, and healing. This can be done regularly and helps greatly for the healing that we all seek.

Offerings

Sometimes we need to do something physical in order to feel as though we are connected to others. We feel that by giving something, even symbolically, we can begin to connect to our ancestors in a physical way.

For example, offerings are one such way we might do this. By offering consecrated wine and bread to God, the Christian faith connects with their spiritual ancestors.

We too can offer consecrated water and food to those who have gone before us, to allow us to give thanks for their lessons and for their presence in our lives. On certain holidays in the Pagan tradition, plates of food are left out for ancestors, in celebration of their help and to show that they are welcome to visit.

Offerings can be done simply by pouring water into the earth, or preparing a complete plate for your ancestors before sitting down to a meal. The food can then be given to the wildlife in your area or put in the compost bin at the end of your meal.

In some Hindu and Buddhist Traditions, it is important to offer consecrated incense, light, water, and food items—ones that have been offered to God or the Buddha first—then there will be great spiritual benefit for the ancestors as they advance eventually becoming illuminated and saintly beings. Then these powerful spiritual influences will enhance your life in wonderful ways.

Incense

As some people relate to the smell of incense as being holy and sacred, it makes sense that you might use it in your own practice of ancestral connecting and healing. If you don't already use incense in your religion or spirituality, you might want to find a supply to keep on hand in your home.

By lighting a stick of incense or a cone you can begin to remember your ancestors and actively bless them.

The connection you make with your ancestors allows you to continue to include them in your life, no matter how many generations have come before you and no matter how many generations might need healing.

Candles

We celebrate many events in our lives with candles, so it makes sense to use candles as well in our personal practice of connecting with our ancestors. You might want to incorporate candles into your daily routine, giving yourself a few moments each day to connect with those who came before you.

You might want to have these candles in a particular place and create a sort of ritual around the use of these candles. Or you might find that lighting these candles on certain holidays that pertain to your ancestors is a good way to connect and to heal past rifts or dissention.

Candles are easy to find and to purchase, or you might want to use candles you already have in your home, depending on what calls to you and depending on what you consider being powerful.

Altars

Some people find that it's best to use some sort of altar space where they can 'meet' with ancestors regularly. In this place, they might keep things like pictures and candles, while also setting up a space for offerings or to simply sit and talk or pray with their ancestors.

An altar can also be as simple as a gathering of special rocks or a plant or even an urn from a relative who has passed. The point is not how big the altar is or how elaborates but how it connects to you and to your understanding of your past.

You might want to include a family tree in this area to help you remember where your past relatives have come from and how this impacts your life today.

Facilitating Ancestral Connections on Your Own

When making an offering of light and incense, begin by making your offering to God/The Buddha/Enlightened Nature and then offering those consecrated items to the ancestors.

In doing so, you are purifying your connection and allowing for spiritual evolution of these connections. This can have dramatic effects on the family in the present.

Conclusion

Across cultures and religions, ancestral ties unite us. Not only do they bind families and cultures to each other, giving us our physical identities and shaping the canvas on which we paint our individual lives, but they are a common thread throughout humanity—a link which in some ways makes us more alike than different.

For many religions these ancestral ties are not severed at death, simply redefined. Our forefathers and mothers go before us to prepare a place in the next life as well as guide our actions in this life.

We begin the Ancestral Healing process by making a personal vow to reconnect with our ancestors through a variety of methods from rituals to prayer. We can energize the process with Divine power, lasting love, and a lifetime of happiness with a little extra help from Joseph.

No matter how you come to the process, it's a chance to strengthen our personal connection with our ancestors. It is an act of love for those who watch over us and a way for them to resolve issues from their time on earth. It is also a way to show love for ourselves, by releasing patterns which no longer suit us. In both cases Ancestral Healing provides the gateway to a deeper, clearer spiritual path, and existence full of pure joy and synchronicity with the universe.

Appendix 1

Sacred Ecology 33

The non-profit organization, Sacred Ecology 33 (SE33) was created not only to teach individuals how to achieve a state of pure happiness, but also to bring humanity together to support each other in living more spiritually integrated lives, and in doing so positively influence the environment.

Why do depression, sadness, and despair seem to permeate so much of the world, if we were put on earth to be happy? Most modern societies condition us to approach life from a negative viewpoint—concentrating on what we don't have, instead of the abundance surrounding us; because we are all interconnected, that negative energy often takes a toll on us, our loved ones, animals, and the environment.

While that may seem overwhelming at first, the good news is personal happiness is available to anyone who is ready to open their hearts and minds. SE33 is a loving, nurturing organization dedicated to the harmony of all those who are ready to change themselves and doing so, better the planet. By holistically cleansing the inner pollution of personal life, individuals can naturally and spontaneously change the outer ecology of the world.

The journey begins with shedding the obstacles which keep us from realizing our true selves. SE33, founder, Joseph Knapp, says that when we, as individuals, communities, or even nations, experience suffering in isolation, we are often left without hope and rely on limited, egocentric solutions. We have lost sight of what truly causes suffering, and fail to recognize the roles we play through selfish actions, as well as inactivity—thus creating a cyclic pattern of constant emptiness. At a global level such behaviour manifests in the rapid and progressive destruction of the environment.

J. T. a store manager from Venice, California says one session with Joseph and she was hooked. *"The room filled with white light so thick I could hardly see through it! (Gads!) I experienced a feeling of divine ecstasy so strong it brought me to tears. The spiritual healing work has taken me beyond my 'small mind' into a vaster 'knowing'. Since the sessions I have been consistently calmer, more aware, and joyous in my everyday life. I am thankful for your work, and that you are making it available."*

Sacred Ecology 33 reminds us, that at our core level, we are all connected or entrained with the greater flow of life, each other, and the Divine. Even western science, which operates on the principle that something must be measured in order to exist, confirms this invisible force of interconnection and influencing rhythm; when several pendulum clocks are hung on the same wall, they synchronize in a matter of days; when animal hearts are placed side by side in science labs, their beats correlate; and when women work in close quarters their fertility cycles align. Therefore, whether we are aware of our influences or not, this connection to each other and the universe is deeply ingrained within each of us.

Joan G. describes an energy healing Joseph provided when she invited him to attend a research session for executives of a national healthcare company. *The energy of the entire group in the room just went to a much higher energy level. Later we heard that some people did actually have an experience that evening and shift in their outlook, and others attending experienced much deeper spiritual connections too. Again, very powerful!"*

Sacred Ecology 33 uses joy to open the door to a new way of living, and offers individuals a chance to view the world with clarity, wisdom and discernment. Joseph helps individuals reach this newfound state of bliss through a method called Clear Light Transmission. The process works by cutting through karmic blocks and emotional clutter, quickening spiritual evolution and propelling the open-hearted to exalted levels of unconditional love, as well as realization of one's own true nature and the world around them.

SE33's focus is on that which is sustainable from an eco-spiritual view, becoming fully conscious of the intimate connections and intricate dependencies existing between living organisms and their environment and acting in ways that do not exploit them.

These quantum breakthroughs to uplift humanity are accomplished through promoting world prayer, establishing retreat centers which offer support, education, and programs for groups and individuals, and tours offering community service through free Sacred Transmissions, teachings and healings. In addition Sacred Ecology promotes its agenda of peace and bliss through books and articles on living happier, healthier, more spiritual lives.

Actor, Madelon Guinazzo from Chicago, Illinois writes of her experience through SE33

At the point that Joseph came into my life there was a culminating affect. It was like the scales tipped and the balance in me between fear and sadness on one end of the scale and love and joy and peace on the other. I experienced an opening up and availability. It was like the ball began rolling away from fear and sadness and toward love and peace. Once this happened it just kept picking up speed. So many things came into my life.

The wisdom gained through SE33 works for anyone because, we are all pure energy. Science describes energy as that which cannot be created or destroyed, which always was, always will be—it changes form, but always exists. In the same manner, theologians describe the Divine as that which cannot be created or destroyed, always was and always will be. Therefore, the Divine is in each of us, and we are a pure drop of eternally existing conscious bliss, we just have forgotten how to be our true selves.

Appendix 2

Who is Joseph?

Even as a young child, Joseph was drawn to the mystical life. At the age of four, he experienced a profound awakening. This experience became the divine spark that guided him to a life of deeply committed spiritual practice.

The breadth of his work comes from a life dedicated to this self-transformation. He embodies the essence of Divine Love through his deep dedication and devotion to God. His work awakens the heart to experience Divine Grace...the source of all transformation, healing and release from one's negative patterns. The more one works with Joseph the more one's consciousness evolves towards the experience of profound Realization, the infusion of Spirit into one's life, and the establishment of a deeper connection to God.

Joseph's self-transformation has come about through over three and a half decades of deep and concentrated spiritual practice rooted in Eastern Yogic and Tibetan Buddhist traditions. Through deep Yogic accomplishment he attained mastery in Kundalini and Shakti-Pat Transmission (touch of Divine Energy). He has also completed more than twelve years of retreat practice in India and Nepal and independent study under the guidance of realized masters including Baba Hari Dass, His Holiness the Dalai Lama, Dilgo Khyenste

Rinpoche, and most importantly his beloved Guru Sri Sri 1008 Kisori-Kisoranand Baba Tinkudi Gosvami, one of the great Siddha Saints of India.

In 1979, Joseph became a fully ordained Vaishnava Priest and was later blessed with carrying on the tradition as a lineage holder, bestowed on him by his Guru. Deeply inspired and required to uphold his commitment as a lineage holder, Joseph continues to maintain his integrity by infusing these sanctified traditions throughout his work.

His love and devotion for his Teacher created a strong bond in him. When Joseph was living in India, he once fell ill and came close to death. In that moment balancing between life and death, his Gurudev blessed and healed him. Through this healing transmission, Baba (his blessed Guru) transferred to Joseph the profound ability to burn-up others' negative karma. This gift is now used to relieve others of their karmic burdens...purifying the psycho-physical field (body, mind, soul) and making them ready to support the Realization of Self and God.

Maintaining a great interest in the power of healing and sacred energy, he later re-visited his studies in Mystic Christianity, Hawaiian Spirituality and Healing, Toltec Shamanism and among other honors, was awarded an honorary diploma of Shaman from don Alejandro (a second generation Peruvian Shaman). Joseph received his Bachelors Degree in Humanistic / Transpersonal Psychology from Sonoma State University and completed graduate work at The Transpersonal Center of Holistic Integration in Southern

California, USA, (and is now working on completing his Ph.D.).

Joseph's dynamic approach fuses the two sciences of Yogic Transmission and Life Systems in the Healing Arts making it possible for one to fully experience the power of Divinity. The core of the work embodies ancient spiritual healing practices combined with thousands of years of wisdom passed down from one lineage holder to another through his Yogic tradition.

His intention is to divinely support those who work with him by unveiling their Sacred Identity of pure consciousness, joy and love while they simultaneously receive profound spiritual healings. This integrated approach causes an intrinsic quickening of one's holistic journey toward achieving a rich, fulfilling life, optimal health and well-being, and Realization of one's True Nature in Liberated Love of God.

When not in retreat, Joseph's work can be experienced through distance healing and phone sessions, and in various centers in the United States with special engagements in Canada, Europe and India.

Services Joseph Offers

- Ancestral Healing
- Clear Light Transmission
- Deity Transmission
- Distance Healing
- Divine Mother Transmission
- Hands On Healing
- Healing Apprenticeship
- Karma Clearing Sessions
- Meditation-Sacred Healing Intensives
- Sacred Energy Healing
- Space Clearing

APPENDIX 3

PATH OF THE SACRED HEALER

Many self-help experts and new age gurus give inspiring presentations and write wonderful, feel-good books, but Joseph Knapp takes things a step further with *Path of the Sacred Healer*. He not only spreads feel-good energy and inspiration, but also provides transformational healing and teaches you to heal yourself through a miraculous five step course known as *Path of the Sacred Healer*.

Path of the Sacred Healer is a once in a lifetime experience to bring clarity, peace, and happiness into your life and help you realize your true potential as a joyful, loving, and empowered human being.

These unique courses in higher living are offered over a period of three to four years. *Path of the Sacred Healer* awakens the dormant part of your spirit through resolving past issues, creating a new momentum for dynamic and balanced spiritual growth, and building a strong foundation to experience self as a sacred being on sacred ground.

In the hustle and bustle of everyday living we often become ungrounded and disconnected with the earth—a naturally healing energy. Add to that the emotional heartbreaks, physical traumas, and general overload of life and it's no wonder people often lose touch with their true selves. Simply put when all those conditions are present the body is not set up to receive spiritual energy because its channels to the Divine are blocked.

In the first level of *Path of the Sacred Healer*, known as 'Peace', Joseph works with you to reconnect with the earth so the body functions as it should. During the intensive two-day, weekend workshop Joseph cleanses your subtle and physical systems and infuses them with the first steps towards spiritual awakening.

Once negativity has been cleared you are easily able to bring new positive energy into your system, receive greater amounts of Divine Love and Sacred Energy, and create a solid foundation for balanced spiritual growth.

Time varies from several weeks to a couple months between the workshops and is designed to give students a chance to effectively practice the new techniques gained during each level.

The second level known as 'Love' concentrates on intensive ancestral healing. Ancestral healing is an exceptional gift to 'burn up' the negative karma of our family lines. Joseph is one of an elite few world-wide, who offers his services to the public. He not only teaches you how to do your own ancestral healings, but guides you through the process of creating one or more luminaries in your ancestral lines. Luminaries are deceased relatives, who have been cleared of their own karma and become illuminated to powerfully assist you in the dynamic cleansing of your whole ancestral line going back hundreds of generations. Once created, these guides work as essential allies moving your spiritual process forward by quantum leaps.

Jeanmarie Reynolds, a psychotherapist from St. Louis, Missouri had this to say about her luminary experience: *My mother actually told me, for the first time that I can remember, that she loved me. That was out of the clear blue at the end of a conversation. So I thought, this must really work! The relationship with her has continued to improve tremendously!*

Once students have mastered the second level of *the Sacred Healer* they often report improved synchronicity in their lives and a new level of direction, confidence, and empowerment.

The ancient Hawaiian process of forgiveness, known as Ho'Oponopono plays a strong role in 'Power', the third level on *The Path*. The word Ho'Oponopono means 'to make it right' either ancestrally or with current relationships you have with others, yourself, places and circumstances, also with God or the Divine. When we cleanse these relationships and clear negativity through forgiveness, we ultimately heal ourselves and open up the path to greater prosperity, not only in relationships, but in all aspects of life from health to finances to spirituality. During this workshop Joseph reveals the powerful transformation techniques that can be used 24 hours a day as you learn the secrets to clearing karma for yourself and others.

'Joy' is celebrated at the fourth level on the *Path of the Sacred Healer* as you delve deeper into your spiritual awakening, concentrating on intensive mediation practice. In addition, Joseph works closely with you through a serious of individual sacred energy healings, Shakti-pat (Sacred Touch), and ancestral healings to remove obstacles that may hinder your ability to create a tangible relationship with the Divine.

Reverend Patricia Jordan from St. Louis, Missouri was deeply moved by her experience. *All that I can tell you is that the Transmission of the Clear Light of God was recognizable for me as Shakti that was being transmitted. I felt open, expanded, and it was a moving and sacred experience.*

Like building blocks, each level on *The Path* must be mastered before another can be attained.

The last level in the journey, 'Bliss' is an extraordinary opportunity reserved for those devoted to spiritual experience and realization. During this year-long course, you will be treated to the rare experience of working one on one with Joseph as he acts as a conduit for different manifestations of the Divine. During the Deity Transmissions, these manifestations extend their pure sacred energy, healing your mind, body and soul and infusing you with higher knowledge. This allows you to build lasting loving relationships with God and others throughout your life, providing more fulfilling levels of health, happiness, and spiritual intimacy.

Joseph's teachings and healings have helped me to release limiting life patterns that once kept me in a constant state of suffering. Now my experiences with life take on greater meaning and purpose with a more profound appreciation for the gift of Divine

Grace, writes Lynn Shook and executive consultant from Kernville, California.

The journey to true peace and lasting happiness is only a click away with *Path of the Sacred Healer* at www.pathofthesacredhealer.org .

Appendix 4

Selected Miracles of Spiritual Intervention

Most of us have a list of emergency contacts in case there's a fire or household accident. But who do you call when there's a spiritual emergency, or the odds seemed so stacked against you, that only a miracle can fix your problems? If a number like that existed, wouldn't you want to keep it in your wallet?

The thing about miracles is that they can happen at anytime, anywhere when we most need them. Ask.com defines a miracle as *an event that appears inexplicable by the laws of nature and so is held to be supernatural in origin or an act of God.*

Over the years Joseph Knapp has had the privilege of facilitating many miracles through his work, whether it be Clear Light Transmission, Ancestral Healing, Karma Clearing, Shakti-pat (Divine Touch), or Deity Transmission, just to name a few.

Sometimes the miracles seemingly happen overnight such as in the case of J.R. from Pacific Palisades, California who called Joseph for a distance healing on his pregnant wife. The baby was in a posterior position, making for a difficult if not dangerous birth. Joseph preformed spiritual intervention work on the mother and child and the baby corrected its position, easily entering the world without complications.

Other times miracles happen more slowly through everyday magic. Joseph fondly recalls the case of James Max Boyer, who eventually became a student, client, and friend. Joseph first met James many years ago and could feel his deep despair across a large room. James was an American-born, Tibetan Buddhist practitioner. He had also been heavily medicated for 17 years due to bipolar disorder. The drugs needed to keep him functioning kept him physically alive, but quelled his spirit to the point of sadness and depression. His physical appearance suffered because he didn't care to bathe or brush his teeth. Though he knew he needed help, he sadly declined when Joseph offered assistance—no one had ever been able to help him. He felt it was his burden to accept the cards he'd been dealt and simply try to exist as best he could.

Not wanting to be intrusive, Joseph respected James' wishes and left. Over the years, Joseph occasionally saw James at various Buddhist gatherings. James often acted out and was in obvious pain, but still rejected help. Then one day ten years later, Joseph ran into James again and reminded him his offer to help still stood. This time the two exchanged phone numbers. Within a few days James called. Joseph learned that James was living in a dingy basement apartment that often overflowed with the sewage from the units above. As soon as they began doing karma clearing and sacred energy sessions, James reported feeling much better and began taking daily showers. Encouraged, he agreed to work with Joseph for a year.

Soon he was able to get a new job and a new car. A new apartment followed within months and his health started to return. Time flew by and before Joseph realized it a year had passed. Looking back he was surprised by all that had been accomplished. But it was James who announced the nearly invisible miracle. He was finally happy! After 17 years of manic, depressive existence, not only was he able to feel normal again, he actually felt pure joy and happiness.

Over the years Joseph's work has been recognized by doctors, therapists, and chiropractors, who often refer clients for supplemental work or when they are having difficulty diagnosing or pinpointing a patient's malady.

Once, a client (who wanted to remain anonymous) came to Joseph with severe pain. Her doctors had tried everything to isolate the source, but nothing seemed to work. During her visit with Joseph he was able to describe the area of her neck that was causing the disturbance. She took the information back to her doctors and they were able to quickly find the problem and provide the needed treatment.

In another case, a wealthy man from Texas had an unbearable pain in his head. He'd been to every specialist in the country without results and spent over $100 thousand on alternative medicine without any relief. In Los Angeles he met a chiropractor who was able to bring his pain on a scale of one to ten with ten being the worst, down to an eight. Encouraged he worked with the chiropractor for several months, but never saw any more improvement. Realizing he could do no more for the man, the chiropractor recommended he visit Joseph. Joseph was able to bring the pain threshold dramatically down to a three. After several sessions Joseph was instructed through divine communication to tell the man that he had taken him as far as they could go together. The man had to take responsibility for the final step in his healing. Divinity told Joseph to tell his client the key to clearing the rest of the pain was for him to go and uplift the souls of terminally ill children by playing music and singing. When the man heard that, he laughed with relief and said, "I used to do that". The pain had just distracted him from a gift he'd given so freely in the past!

Jonathan Shook who lived in the Chicago suburbs met Joseph after being diagnosed by several different doctors with dilated cardiomyopathy, a heart condition in which the blood going through the organ was very, very slow due to muscle damage.

My family physician was hosting Joseph one night at his office with other patients of his attending; I remember when Joseph was working on my heart. I definitely felt something was happening. There was what seemed like warmth in my chest, then a pain and then tightness and then more pain. Then I started having quickness of breath. Then I was caught up in the whole experience of wondering was I having a heart attack? I realized I was in the presence of a doctor, in a doctor's office and I realized no I wouldn't be having a heart attack from what had just happened. So I realized in my conscious mind that it's okay, don't worry it's just whatever Joseph could do or provide... it happened. The healing happened at that one time.

A short time later Jonathan went back to the cardiologist and received an astonishing positive evaluation, it seemed what is usually permanent muscle damage had been undone. The doctor asked him what he'd done differently. *I told him about the experience with Joseph. And I said, "Do you think this hands on healing made this improvement possible and have you ever experienced this?" He thought it was possible and I was fortunate that I was able to receive healing other than traditional drug therapy or surgery. I really experienced some profound healing that was documented. I know I must always remain grateful. I experienced a miracle!*

So the next time your spirit or body needs a miracle, why wait until all other avenues are exhausted, when a trustworthy and amazing healer is ready to help? The next time you have a spiritual, emotional or physical problem, know that you have a miracle emergency contact number with a direct line to Joseph Knapp.

Contact Information for Joseph Knapp

For more information feel free to contact Joseph at:

1-877-838-1133

or visit his websites:

www.sacredecology33.org

and

www.pathofthesacredhealer.org

BIBLIOGRAPHY

Adamski, M. (2002). "Memorial Day helps families stay connected with ancestors." Retrieved 4/25/2009 from http://archives.starbulletin.com/2002/05/25/features/story1.html

Belanger, J. (2007). *The ghost files.* (Career Press).

DeCaroli, R. (2004). *Haunting the Buddha: Indian popular religions and the formation of Buddhism.* (Oxford University Press US).

Holman Bible Dictionary. "Ancestors." http://studylight.org/dic/hbd/view.cgi?numberT327

Jacobs, Joseph. "Ancestor Worship." http://www.jewishencyclopedia.com

Knipe, R. (1989). *The water of life.* (University of Hawaii Press).

Lim, D. and de Neui, P. (2006). *Communicating Christ in the Buddhist world.* (William Carey Library).

Maeda, T. (1976). "Ancestor worship in Japan" in Newell, W. (1976), *Ancestors.* (Walter de Gruyter).

Mathews, P. and Foster, L. (2005). *Handbook to life in the ancient Maya world*. (Oxford University Press US).

Michaels, A. and Harshav, B. (2004). *Hinduism: past and present*. (Princeton University Press).

Ooms, H. (1967). "The Religion of the Household," in *Contemporary religions in Japan*, vol. VIII, nos. 3-4, September-December 1967.

Paper, J. (2007). *Native North American religious traditions*. (Greenwood Publishing Group).

Peregrine, P. et al. (2001). *Encyclopedia of Prehistory*. (Springer).

Renard, J. (2002). *101 Questions and answers on Confucianism, Daoism and Shinto*. (Paulist Press).

Smith, J. (1974). *Ancestor worship in contemporary Japan*. (Stanford University Press).

Stuart, J. et al. (2001). *Worshipping the ancestors*. (Stanford University Press).

"Sufism" http://en.wikipedia.org/wiki/Sufism

Walls, J. (2007). *The Oxford handbook of eschatology*. (Oxford University Press).

Woodhead, L. (2002). *Religions in the modern world.* (Routledge).

Yalae, P. (2008). *Neo-Africanism.* (Trafford Publishing).

www.ingramcontent.com/pod-product-compliance
Lightning Source LLC
Chambersburg PA
CBHW060340080526
44584CB00013B/845